A – Alarm to wake up: Encourage to wake up early and play to promote a healthy, active lifestyle.

B - Brushing Teeth: Instill the habit of brushing teeth at least twice a day for good oral hygiene.

C - Cleanliness: Teach the importance of cleanliness, including washing hands regularly and keeping personal spaces tidy.

D - Drinking Water: Promote the habit of staying hydrated by drinking an adequate amount of water daily.

E - Empathy: Encourage empathy and kindness towards others, fostering positive social interactions

F - Family Time: Stress the significance of spending quality time with family for bonding and support

G - Gratitude: Teach the habit of expressing gratitude to cultivate a positive and appreciative mindset

H - Healthy Eating: Promote a balanced diet with fruits, vegetables, and nutritious meals for overall well-being

I – Importance: Foster the importance of every activity responsibility and decision-making

J - Journaling: Introduce the habit of journaling or expressing thoughts and feelings through writing or drawing.

K - Kindness: Instill the value of being kind and considerate towards others

L - Listening: Teach the importance of active listening in communication to enhance understanding.

M - Mindfulness: Introduce mindfulness practices to help children stay present and manage stress.

N - Napping: Emphasize the importance of sufficient sleep and the benefits of taking regular naps.

O - Outdoor Play: Encourage outdoor play and exploration to support physical and cognitive development

P - Politeness: Teach good manners and the habit of being polite and respectful in various situations.

Q - Questioning: Promote curiosity and the habit of asking questions to facilitate learning

R - Reading: Cultivate a love for reading by making it a regular and enjoyable habit.

S - Sharing: Encourage the habit of sharing with others to build a sense of community and generosity

T - Time Management: Teach basic time management skills, helping children prioritize tasks and responsibilities.

U - Unplugging: Promote the habit of taking breaks from screens and engaging in screen-free activities

V - Values: Instill strong values like honesty, integrity, and responsibility in children

W - Well-being: Emphasize the importance of overall well-being, including physical, mental, and emotional health.

X - eXploring: Encourage a sense of exploration and curiosity to broaden children's perspectives

Y - Yoga: Introduce simple yoga or mindfulness exercises for relaxation and focus.

Z - Zeal for Learning: Foster a passion for learning by making education an exciting and continuous journey.

Hi Children,

I express heartfelt gratitude to all for diligently following good habits and being true superheroes in making positive choices.

Loving & Caring

Spiderman.....

Made in the USA
Columbia, SC
23 March 2024

33520518R00015